Contents:

Answers and Mark Schemes

From the founder of Exam Ninja...

Thank you for choosing to buy these Key Stage 2 practice papers by Exam Ninja!

I founded Exam Ninja several years ago with the core purpose of helping children of all ages to do the best they possibly can in their exams. I sincerely hope that this book helps your child achieve their potential in their KS2 SATs.

Exams (like ninjas) are pretty scary things, and so whether it's Key Stage 1, Key Stage 2 or Key Stage 3 SATs tests, Phonics Screening Checks, 11+ exams or GCSEs your child is preparing for, Exam Ninja has the resources they need.

Joshua Geake
Founder and Director of Exam Ninja.

We view exams and tests as an opportunity for your child to show just how talented and special they are. With our resources and a little help and support from you, we can enable them to approach their assessments positively and confidently. We know they can do it!

So from me and everyone at Exam Ninja – good luck for the KS2 SATs in May!

How these tests will help your child

We have devised these Key Stage 2 practice papers to be used at any time throughout the year to provide practice for the Key Stage 2 SATs tests.

As your child works through these tests, they will gain invaluable practice in answering challenging KS2 SATs questions. As our many tens of thousands of customers will tell you: Exam Ninja's resources work! In 2013, 2014 and 2015, over 80% of our customers' children achieved level 5 or more in **all** of their KS2 SATs tests and in

2016, over 80% got a scaled score in excess of 100! Through the use of these practice papers, we believe these results will get even better!

After completing the tests, you will be able to check how well your child has performed and gain a better awareness of their strengths and weaknesses. Once you have identified a weakness, this can be tackled head on with our targeted KS2 SATs packs. See **ExamNinja.co.uk** for more details.

Exam.Ninja

© Exam Ninja

Taking the tests

Before your child starts a test, check that everything is prepared for the test to run smoothly:

- Provide a **quiet environment** that's free from distractions such as televisions, smartphones and music players so that children can complete the tests undisturbed.

- Ensure they feel **relaxed and unhurried** when starting the tests. For example, don't start a test just before bedtime or before their favourite television programme!

- They will need the following equipment for the **English Reading and Grammar, Punctuation and Spelling papers**: a pen, pencil and a rubber. **For the Maths tests they will need:** a pen, pencil, rubber, ruler and protractor (angle measurer).

- The amount of time given for each test **varies**, so always check the first page of the paper before your child starts.

- Check your child has asked all the questions they need to ask about the test **before** it begins.

- As part of this book we have provided the audio for the **Spelling Papers** as a **FREE** download. We highly recommend that you use it to provide a very realistic KS2 SATs exam environment.

Be strict about the amount of time you allocate to your child when they take these tests and ensure that they don't leave their seat or ask any questions once a test has begun.

Marking the tests

Once your child has completed a test you can mark it by using the included **Answers and Mark Schemes** booklet. Exam markers do try to award pupils as many marks as they can but they rarely give them the benefit of the doubt, so ensure that you mark their papers **honestly** and **without any bias**.

Within each **Answers and Mark Scheme** section you will find a table to fill in with your child's marks. Take the time to fill these in to keep a record of how they're performing.

Levels and Scaled Scores

Pupils used to be awarded a 'level', such as '3b' or '4c', however for 2016, levels were replaced with 'scaled scores'. **Scaled scores** are simply a different way of reporting your child's exam marks. Instead of being given their marks and a level, their marks will be converted into a scaled score.

Children whose scaled score is close to 100 are judged to have reached the national standard that's expected of them. Those scoring over 100 will have performed above that standard, whilst those that score below 100 have not reached the expected standard.

KEY STAGE 2
MATHEMATICS TESTS

ANSWERS & MARK SCHEMES

About the KS2 Maths Practice Papers

There are three **full** sets of **KS2 Maths Practice Papers**. Each set of KS2 Maths Practice Papers consists of three separate papers: **Paper 1 (Arithmetic), Paper 2 (Reasoning)** and **Paper 3 (Reasoning).** Calculators are **strictly not allowed** for **any** of these tests.

 This pencil sign means that an answer needs to be written either where indicated by the pencil or in the position instructed in the question.

Some questions will have an answer box that says "Show your working". Children should use this space to write out their working and their final answer in the smaller box within it. This way, even if a child ultimately gets the answer wrong, they could still be awarded marks for approaching it in the right way.

Paper 1 (Arithmetic)

Paper 1 lasts for **30 minutes** and is out of a total of **40 marks**.

Paper 2 (Reasoning) and Paper 3 (Reasoning)

Paper 2 and Paper 3 each last for **40 minutes** and have a total of **35 marks** each.

Marking and Assessing

Once your child has completed a test, mark it using the **Answers and Mark Schemes** within this book, add up the marks and enter them in the table below. After completing a full set of papers, add up the scores for Paper 1, Paper 2 and the Paper 3 to get a total out of **110**.

Maths Marks Table

	SET A	SET B	SET C
Paper 1 (30 mins, out of 40)			
Paper 2 (40 mins, out of 35)			
Paper 3 (40 mins, out of 35)			
Total (out of 110)			

Mathematics - Paper 1 (Arithmetic) Set A Answers

Q	Mark	Answers
1.	1	1,094
2.	1	642
3.	1	9.1
4.	1	130
5.	1	1,844
6.	1	84
7.	1	559
8.	1	2.46
9.	1	2,100
10.	1	58
11.	1	80
12.	1	560
13.	1	$\frac{1}{40}$ *Accept an equivalent fraction or decimal such as* $\frac{2}{80}$ *or 0.025.*
14.	1	59,400
15.	1	5,000,000
16.	1	142
17.	1	260
18.	1	20.32

Q	Mark	Answers
19.	1	$\frac{2}{5}$ *Accept an equivalent fraction or decimal such as* $\frac{4}{10}$ *or 0.4.*
20.	1	14,199
21.	1	701
22.	1	95.98
23.	Up to 2	1,440 *Award **2 marks** for the correct answer.* *Incorrect answer? Award **1 mark** for a correct method which contains no more than one arithmetic error.* ***Do not** award a mark if the error is in the place value.* ***Do not** award a mark if the final answer is missing.*
24.	1	5.65
25.	Up to 2	322 *Award **2 marks** for the correct answer.* *Incorrect answer? Award **1 mark** for a correct method which contains no more than one arithmetic error.* *Award **1 mark** for a correct short-division method only if there is evidence of carrying figures.* ***Do not** award a mark if the final answer is missing.*
26.	1	$\frac{2}{5}$ *Accept an equivalent fraction or decimal such as* $\frac{4}{10}$ *or 0.4.*
27.	1	342
28.	1	275,054
29.	Up to 2	15,363 *Award **2 marks** for the correct answer.* *Incorrect answer? Award **1 mark** for a correct method which contains no more than one arithmetic error.* ***Do not** award a mark if the error is in the place value.* ***Do not** award a mark if the final answer is missing.*

Exam Ninja

Q	Mark	Answers
30.	1	21
31.	1	38
32.	1	$\frac{3}{11}$ or 0.27 **Do not** award a mark if the decimal is rounded or truncated. There must be evidence that the digits 2 and 7 is a recurring pattern.
33.	1	$1\frac{1}{24}$ Accept an equivalent fraction or decimal such as $\frac{25}{24}$ or $1\frac{2}{48}$ or 1.0416. **Do not** award a mark if the decimal is rounded or truncated. There must be evidence that the digit 6 is a recurring digit.
34.	Up to 2	53 Award **2 marks** for the correct answer. Incorrect answer? Award **1 mark** for a correct method which contains no more than one arithmetic error. Award **1 mark** for a correct short-division method only if there is evidence of carrying figures. **Do not** award a mark if the final answer is missing.
35.	1	$1\frac{3}{8}$ Accept an equivalent fraction or decimal such as $\frac{11}{8}$ or $1\frac{6}{16}$ or 0.375.
36.	1	100

Mathematics - Paper 1 (Arithmetic) Set B Answers

Q	Mark	Answers
1.	1	337
2.	1	476
3.	1	12.1
4.	1	170
5.	1	3,300
6.	1	807
7.	1	130
8.	1	5
9.	1	144
10.	1	$\dfrac{2}{11}$ Accept an equivalent fraction or decimal such as $\dfrac{4}{22}$ or $0.\overline{18}$. **Do not** award a mark if the decimal is rounded or truncated. There must be evidence that the digits 1 and 8 are a recurring pattern.
11.	1	92
12.	1	702.8
13.	1	3.33
14.	1	34,940
15.	1	250,000
16.	1	242
17.	1	360
18.	1	32.04

Exam Ninja

Q	Mark	Answers
19.	1	$6\frac{5}{9}$ Accept an equivalent fraction or decimal such as $\frac{59}{9}$ or $6\frac{10}{18}$ or $6.\dot{5}$. **Do not** award a mark if the decimal is rounded or truncated. There must be evidence that the 5 is a recurring digit.
20.	1	12,680
21.	1	601
22.	1	25.03
23.	Up to 2	79.9 Award **2 marks** for the correct answer. Incorrect answer? Award **1 mark** for a correct method which contains no more than one arithmetic error. **Do not** award a mark if the error is in the place value. **Do not** award a mark if the final answer is missing.
24.	1	16.85
25.	Up to 2	317 Award **2 marks** for the correct answer. Incorrect answer? Award **1 mark** for a correct method which contains no more than one arithmetic error. Award **1 mark** for a correct short-division method only if there is evidence of carrying figures. **Do not** award a mark if the final answer is missing.
26.	1	$\frac{11}{16}$ Accept an equivalent fraction or decimal such as $\frac{22}{32}$ or 0.6875.
27.	1	$8\frac{1}{2}$ Accept an equivalent fraction or decimal such as 8.5 or $8\frac{25}{50}$.
28.	1	117,065

Q	Mark	Answers
29.	Up to 2	36,408 Award **2 marks** for the correct answer. Incorrect answer? Award **1 mark** for a correct method which contains no more than one arithmetic error. **Do not** award a mark if the error is in the place value. **Do not** award a mark if the final answer is missing.
30.	1	36
31.	1	34
32.	1	$\dfrac{11}{30}$ Accept an equivalent fraction or decimal such as $\dfrac{22}{60}$ or $0.3\dot{6}$. **Do not** award a mark if the decimal is rounded or truncated. There must be evidence that the 6 is a recurring digit.
33.	1	0.01
34.	Up to 2	41 Award **2 marks** for the correct answer. Incorrect answer? Award **1 mark** for a correct method which contains no more than one arithmetic error. Award **1 mark** for a correct short-division method only if there is evidence of carrying figures. **Do not** award a mark if the final answer is missing.
35.	1	$\dfrac{37}{40}$ Accept an equivalent fraction or decimal such as $\dfrac{74}{80}$ or 0.925.
36.	1	56

Mathematics - Paper 1 (Arithmetic) Set C Answers

Q	Mark	Answers
1.	1	11
2.	1	$\dfrac{7}{20}$ Accept an equivalent fraction or decimal such as $\dfrac{35}{100}$ or 0.35.
3.	1	27
4.	1	1,040
5.	1	5,371
6.	1	0.29
7.	1	501.4
8.	1	12.98
9.	1	1,260
10.	1	648
11.	1	90.2
12.	1	401.6
13.	1	2,847
14.	1	49,900
15.	1	0.001
16.	1	326
17.	1	51
18.	1	69.36

Q	Mark	Answers
19.	1	$\dfrac{4}{5}$ Accept an equivalent fraction or decimal such as $\dfrac{16}{20}$ or 0.8.
20.	1	10,532
21.	1	915
22.	1	46.76
23.	Up to 2	1,330 Award **2 marks** for the correct answer. Incorrect answer? Award **1 mark** for a correct method which contains no more than one arithmetic error. **Do not** award a mark if the error is in the place value. **Do not** award a mark if the final answer is missing.
24.	1	-41.1
25.	1	392
26.	1	425,024
27.	Up to 2	314 Award **2 marks** for the correct answer. Incorrect answer? Award **1 mark** for a correct method which contains no more than one arithmetic error. Award **1 mark** for a correct short-division method only if there is evidence of carrying figures. **Do not** award a mark if the final answer is missing.
28.	1	$\dfrac{5}{12}$ Accept an equivalent fraction or decimal such as $\dfrac{10}{24}$ or $0.41\dot{6}$. **Do not** award a mark if the decimal is rounded or truncated. There must be evidence that the 6 is a recurring digit.

Q	Mark	Answers
29.	Up to 2	39,931 Award **2 marks** for the correct answer. Incorrect answer? Award **1 mark** for a correct method which contains no more than one arithmetic error. **Do not** award a mark if the error is in the place value. **Do not** award a mark if the final answer is missing.
30.	1	56
31.	1	-0.49
32.	1	2
33.	1	$\frac{17}{20}$ Accept an equivalent fraction or decimal such as $\frac{34}{40}$ or 0.85.
34.	Up to 2	205.25 or $205\frac{1}{4}$ Award **2 marks** for the correct answer. Incorrect answer? Award **1 mark** for a correct method which contains no more than one arithmetic error. Award **1 mark** for a correct short-division method only if there is evidence of carrying figures. **Do not** award a mark if the final answer is missing.
35.	1	$1\frac{5}{12}$ Accept an equivalent fraction or decimal such as $\frac{17}{12}$ or $\frac{110}{24}$ or $1.41\dot{6}$. **Do not** award a mark if the decimal is rounded or truncated. There must be evidence that the 6 is a recurring digit.
36.	1	$11\frac{13}{16}$ Accept an equivalent fraction or decimal such as 11.8125 or $11\frac{26}{32}$.

Mathematics - Paper 2 (Reasoning) Set A Answers

Q	Mark	Answers
1.	1	140 162
2.	Up to 2	244 Award **2 marks** for the correct answer. Incorrect answer? Award **1 mark** if there's evidence of a correct method e.g. 8 × 7 = 56 or 300 − 56 = 244.
3.	1 1	Rome 2°C **Do not** accept -2°C.
4.	Up to 2	Award **2 marks** if all **four** shapes have been correctly matched. Incorrect answer? Award **1 mark** if **two** shapes have been correctly matched. **Do not** award a mark for any shape that's been matched to more than one fraction.
5.	1	9 hours 27 minutes
6.	1	5 minutes to ten. Accept any other equivalent answer. 9:55 9:55 am 9:55 pm 21:55
7.	Up to 2	8, 12 or 24 75 150 or 200 Award **2 marks** for **three** correct answers. Incorrect answer? Award **1 mark** if there are **two** correct answers.
8.	1 Up to 2	£3.65 15 apples Award **2 marks** for the correct answer. Incorrect answer? Award **1 mark** if there's evidence of a suitable method e.g. £4.55 − 5p = £4.50 or £4.50 ÷ 30p = 15.

Q	Mark	Answers
9.	Up to 2	 $$\begin{array}{r} 6\ \boxed{7} \\ \times\ \boxed{4}\ 8 \\ \hline 5\ 3\ 6 \\ 2\ 6\ 8\ 0 \\ \hline 3\ 2\ 1\ 6 \end{array}$$ Award **2 marks** for the correct answer. Incorrect answer? Award **1 mark** if there's **one** correct digit.
10.	1 1	Within the range of 7.9cm to 8.3cm. Within the range of 118° to 122°.
11.	1	*The number in the second box should be equal to the number in the first box, plus 1 and then multiplied by 5. E.g. 3, 20 or 8, 45.*
12.	1	1.55
13.	1 1	
14.	1	 *The four hexagons must be a similar shape to the example below to have a perimeter of 28cm.*
15.	Up to 2	102° Award **2 marks** for the correct answer. Incorrect answer? Award **1 mark** if there's evidence of a suitable method. *E.g. 2 × 39 = 78 or 180 − 78 = 102.*

Exam Ninja

Q	Mark	Answers
16.	1	
17.	1	23
	1	19
18.	Up to 2	£5,780 Award **2 marks** for the correct answer. Incorrect answer? Award **1 mark** if there's evidence of a suitable method. E.g. £28.90 ÷ 5 = £5.78 or £5.78 × 1,000 = £5780.
19.	1	Elsie is correct because $\frac{1}{4}$ (or 25%) of 200 is greater than $\frac{1}{2}$ (or 50%) of 50.
20.	Up to 2	175 pages Award **2 marks** for the correct answer. Incorrect answer? Award **1 mark** if there's evidence of a suitable method. E.g. $\frac{4}{7}$ of page total = 100 so page total = 100 × $\frac{7}{4}$ = 175.
21.	Up to 2	87,450 87,400 87,000 90,000 Award **2 marks** for stating **all** the correct answers. Incorrect answer? Award **1 mark** if there are **two** correct answers.

Q	Mark	Answers
1.	1	
2.	Up to 2	£0.90 (accept 90p) Award **2 marks** for the correct answer. Incorrect answer? Award **1 mark** if there's evidence of a correct method e.g. £10 – 10p =£9.90, £9.90 ÷ 11 = 90p.
3.	Up to 3	700cm² Award **3 marks** for the correct answer. Incorrect answer? Award **2 marks** for the correct calculation 45 × 36 = 1,584cm² or if there's evidence of a suitable method with one arithmetic error. Award **1 mark** if there's evidence of a correct method that has more than one arithmetic error. **Do not** award any marks if the error is in the place value of the multiplication.
4.	Up to 2	Award **2 marks** for a correctly filled in table. Incorrect answer? Award **1 mark** if three cells are correctly filled in.
5.	1	

Q	Mark	Answers
6.	1	24 days
7.	1 1	16 (accept 16.0) 10.5
8.	1 1	905 CXXX
9.	Up to 2	A, B and D. Award **2 marks** for the correct answer. Incorrect answer? Award **1 mark** if there are **two** correct letters.
10.	1	21.6
11.	Up to 2	36,550 36,500 37,000 40,000 Award **2 marks** for stating **all** the correct answers. Incorrect answer? Award **1 mark** if there are **two** correct answers.
12.	1 1	41 55
13.	1 1	Trapezium Kite
14.	1 1	12 people Wales
15.	Up to 2	432 cans Award **2 marks** for the correct answer. Incorrect answer? Award **1 mark** if there's evidence of a suitable method with one arithmetic error. E.g. 2 × 18 = 36, 36 × 12 = 432.
16.	1	120°

Q	Mark	Answers
17.	Up to 2	£720 *Award **2 marks** for the correct answer.* *Incorrect answer? Award **1 mark** if there is evidence of a suitable method.* *E.g. 1200 ÷ 25 = 48, 48 × 15 = £720.*
18.	1	$\dfrac{1}{8}$ *(accept answers between* $\dfrac{1}{7}$ *and* $\dfrac{1}{9}$ *)*
	1	75 *(accept answers between 73 and 77)*
19.	Up to 2	450 pupils *Award **2 marks** for the correct answer.* *Incorrect answer? Award **1 mark** if there's evidence of a suitable method. E.g.* $\dfrac{5}{9}$ *of pupil total = 250, page total = 250 ×* $\dfrac{9}{5}$ *= 450.*
20.	1	Aisha is **not** correct because 13 (or another suitable value such as 23 or 43) is not a multiple of 3. ***Do not** award the mark if a suitable example such as 13, 23 or 43 is missing.*

Mathematics - Paper 2 (Reasoning) Set C Answers

Q	Mark	Answers
1.	1 1	70 minutes 10 p.m.
2.	1 1 1	8 sides Pentagon Octagon
3.	1	1 hour 53 minutes 9 seconds
4.	1 1	40m 93.75m^2
5.	1 1 1	2°C 9°C *Accept answers between 9:30am and 9:45am*

6. — Up to 2

Fractions: $\frac{3}{4}$, $\frac{2}{5}$, $\frac{7}{8}$, $\frac{5}{8}$, $\frac{3}{5}$

*Award **2 marks** if all **four** shapes have been correctly matched.*
*Incorrect answer? Award **1 mark** if two shapes have been correctly matched.*
***Do not** award a mark for any shape that's been matched to more than one fraction.*

7. — Up to 2

$$
\begin{array}{r}
9\,2 \\
\times \quad 2\,7 \\
\hline
6\,4\,4 \\
1\,8\,4\,0 \\
\hline
2\,4\,8\,4 \\
\end{array}
$$

*Award **2 marks** for the correct answer.*
*Incorrect answer? Award **1 mark** if there's **one** correct digit.*

Q	Mark	Answers
8.	**Up to 2**	£3.04 *Award **2 marks** for the correct answer.* *Incorrect answer? Award **1 mark** if there's evidence of a suitable method. E.g.* 2 × £1.99 = £3.98, 3 × £3.74 = £11.22, £3.98 + £11.32 = £15.20, £15.20 ÷5 = £3.04.
9.	1	20 cars
10.	1	Award **1 mark** for correctly drawing **all five** lines of symmetry.
11.	1	2 16 9 5, 13
12.	**Up to 2**	36 girls *Award **2 marks** for the correct answer.* *Incorrect answer? Award **1 mark** if there's evidence of a suitable method.* E.g. $\frac{3}{8} \times \frac{2}{3} \times$ number of girls in class = 9, $\frac{3}{8} \times \frac{2}{3} = \frac{1}{4}$, number of girls in class = $9 \div \frac{1}{4} = 36$.
13.	1 1	200ml
14.	1	c = 4b - 2
15.	1 1	5, 29 154

Q	Mark	Answers
16.	1	$\dfrac{3}{14}$
17.	1 1	7 balloons 35km
18.	Up to 2	13.5, 17 *Award **2 marks** for the correct answer.* *Incorrect answer? Award **1 mark** if there's **one** correct number.*
19.	1	+5, ×3, -4, ÷4
20.	Up to 2	 *Incorrect answer? Award **1 mark** if there's one correctly drawn shape element.*

Mathematics - Paper 3 (Reasoning) Set A Answers

Q	Mark	Answers
1.	Up to 2	<table><tr><td></td><td>Multiple of 4</td><td>Not a multiple of 4</td></tr><tr><td>Multiple of 6</td><td>24</td><td>6, 18, 30…</td></tr><tr><td>Not a multiple of 6</td><td>4, 8, 16…</td><td>1, 2, 3, 5…</td></tr></table> Award **2 marks** if the sorting table has been completed correctly. Incorrect answer? Award **1 mark** if **two** cells have been correctly completed.
2.	Up to 2	$\frac{2}{3}$ or an equivalent fraction such as $\frac{8}{12}$. $\frac{3}{4}$ or an equivalent fraction such as $\frac{9}{12}$. Award **2 marks** for **two** correct answers. Incorrect answer? Award **1 mark** if there's **one** correct answer.
3.	1	$1.4, 1\frac{1}{3}$
4.	1 1	October £600
5.	Up to 2	42, -9, -43 Award **2 marks** for the correct answer. Incorrect answer? Award **1 mark** if there are **two** correct values.
6.	Up to 2	×100, ÷1,000 Award **2 marks** for **two** correct answers. Incorrect answer? Award **1 mark** if there is **one** correct answer.
7.	1	Thirty thousand, five hundred and eight.
8.	1	
9.	Up to 2	8.1g Award **2 marks** for the correct answer. Incorrect answer? Award **1 mark** if there's evidence of a suitable method. E.g. 13.5 × 3 = 40.5, 40.5 ÷ 5 = 8.1.

Q	Mark	Answers
10.	Up to 2	£0.17 (accept 17p) Award **2 marks** for the correct answer. Incorrect answer? Award **1 mark** if there's evidence of a suitable method. E.g. 84 ÷ 4 = 21p, 228 ÷ 6 = 38p, 38p − 21p = 17p.
11.	Up to 2	8 [2] 3 [7] − [2] 5 [1] 8 5 7 1 9 Award **2 marks** for the correct answer. Incorrect answer? Award **1 mark** if there are **two** correct values.
12.	1	0.992
13.	Up to 2	$\frac{4}{9} < \frac{2}{3} < \frac{3}{4}$ $\frac{4}{9} < \frac{2}{3} < \frac{5}{6}$ $\frac{4}{9} < \frac{3}{4} < \frac{5}{6}$ $\frac{2}{3} < \frac{3}{4} < \frac{5}{6}$ Award **2 marks** for any **two** of the above expressions. Incorrect answer? Award **1 mark** if there is **one** complete expression.
14.	Up to 2	21 4.2 5 1.05 4 1.25
15.	1	Award **2 marks** for the correct answer. Incorrect answer? Award **1 mark** if there are **two** correct values. Accept **any** of the above.
16.	Up to 2	5.25 Award **2 marks** for the correct answer. Incorrect answer? Award **1 mark** if there's evidence of a suitable method. E.g. 2(number − 3) + 2 = 6.5, 6.5 − 2 = 4.5, 4.5 ÷ 2 = 2.25, 2.25 + 3 = 5.25.

Q	Mark	Answers
17.	1	40%
18.	1	60p, 65p, 72p
19.	1	41, 58
20.	1 1 1	Swimming 5 Netball, basketball
21.	1 1	A = (16, -7) B = (20, -7)

Mathematics - Paper 3 (Reasoning) Set B Answers

Q	Mark	Answers
1.	Up to 2	Award **2 marks** if the Venn diagram has been completed correctly. Incorrect answer? Award **1 mark** if **three** numbers have been correctly placed.
2.	1	-7, -2 Do not accept 7-, 7, 2- or 2.
3.	Up to 2	£10.91 Award **2 marks** for the correct answer. Incorrect answer? Award **1 mark** if there's evidence of a suitable method. E.g. £5.10 + £3.99 = £9.09. £20 - £9.09 = £10.91.
	1	£13.08
4.	Up to 2	44, 46 Award **2 marks** for the correct answer. Incorrect answer? Award **1 mark** if there's **one** correct answer.
5.	1	Fifty-nine thousand and two.
6.	1	
7.	1	0.012kg
	1	75cm
8.	1	

Q	Mark	Answers
9.	Up to 2	75g Award **2 marks** for the correct answer. Incorrect answer? Award **1 mark** if there's evidence of a suitable method. E.g. 650g – 200g = 450g, 450 ÷ 6 = 75g.
10.	1	There are **90** sweets in a bag. **12** friends share them equally. Each friend gets **7** sweets. There are **6** sweets left over. **Or** There are **90** sweets in a bag. **7** friends share them equally. Each friend gets **12** sweets. There are **6** sweets left over.
11.	Up to 2	⑨ 4 ⑥ 9 ⑥ 8 + 4 7 5 ② 3 8 9 Award **2 marks** for the correct answer. Incorrect answer? Award **1 mark** there are **two** correct values.
12.	1	28.43
13.	1	4
14.	Up to 2	8 eggs Award **2 marks** for the correct answer. Incorrect answer? Award **1 mark** if there's evidence of a suitable method. E.g. 3 × (number of eggs) + 6 = 30, 3 × (number of eggs) = 24, number of eggs = $\frac{24}{3}$ = 8.
15.	1	
16.	Up to 2	46 Award **2 marks** for the correct answer. Incorrect answer? Award **1 mark** if there's evidence of a suitable method. E.g. ((number + 50) ÷ 2) – 20 = 28, (number + 50) ÷ 2) = 48, number = 96 – 50 = 46.
17.	1 1	70 700

Q	Mark	Answers
18.	Up to 2	125ml *Award **2 marks** for the correct answer.* *Incorrect answer? Award **1 mark** if there's evidence of a suitable method. E.g.* $$\frac{5}{12} \times 300\text{ml} = 125\text{ml}.$$
19.	Up to 3	2,606.5cm^2 *Award **3 marks** for the correct answer.* *Incorrect answer? Award **2 marks** if there's evidence of the total area being 35 × 75.5 = 2,642.5cm^2.* *Award **1 mark** for a suitable method that includes no more than one arithmetic error.* ***Do not** award any marks if the error is in the place value of the multiplication.*
20.	1 1 1	B = (15, 7) C = (0, -6) Centre = (7.5, 0.5)

Mathematics - Paper 3 (Reasoning) Set C Answers

Q	Mark	Answers
1.	1 1	150g 14%
2.	1 1	36 162
3.	1 1	26,048,000 26.048
4.	Up to 2 1	£40 Award **2 marks** for the correct answer. Incorrect answer? Award **1 mark** if there's evidence of a suitable method. E.g. £1.65 + £3.35 = £5.00, £5.00 ÷ 8 = £40. £0.40 (accept 40p)
5.	Up to 2	27km Award **2 marks** for the correct answer. Incorrect answer? Award **1 mark** if there's evidence of a suitable method. E.g. 4 × unit distance = 36, unit distance = 9km, distance = 3 × unit distance = 27km.
6.	1	
7.	1	0.4g, 0.3kg, $\dfrac{1}{3}$ kg, 450g, 500g
8.	1 1	37 minutes 9 minutes

Exam Ninja

Q	Mark	Answers
9.	1	
10.	1 1	28 48
11.	1 1	3.8cm 1.4cm
12.	Up to 2	$$\begin{array}{c}2\ \boxed{4}\ 6\ 3\\ +\ \boxed{1}\ 4\ \boxed{7}\ \boxed{9}\\ \hline 3\ 9\ 4\ 2\end{array}$$ Award **2 marks** for the correct answer. Incorrect answer? Award **1 mark** if there are **two** correct values.
13.	1	0.6
14.	1	
15.	1	
16.	1	Award **1 mark** for either of the two example right-angled triangles shown or **any** other right-angled triangle.

Q	Mark	Answers

17. | Up to 2 |

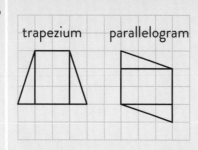

trapezium   parallelogram

Award **1 mark** for **each** correctly drawn shape.
Do not award a mark if the shape(s) are not labelled.

18. | Up to 2 |

Month	Sunny Days	Wet Days
May	12	16
June	14	8
July	18	6
August	16	8
September	14	10
October	10	18

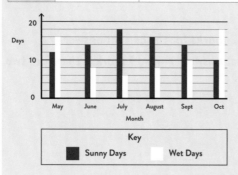

Award **2 marks** for a correctly completed table and chart.
Incorrect answer? Award **1 mark** if either the table **or** the chart is correctly completed.

| 1 | 12 |

19. | Up to 2 | 2.965m
Award **2 marks** for the correct answer.
Incorrect answer? Award **1 mark** if there's evidence of a suitable method. E.g.
1.2m - 92cm = 28cm, 1.2m + 92cm + 28cm = 2.4m, 240cm + (2 × 28.25cm) = 296.5cm
= 2.965m.

20. | Up to 2 |

	Number of flat surfaces	Number of curved surfaces
Sphere	0	1
Cone	1	1
Cylinder	2	1
Cube	6	0

Award **2 marks** for a correctly completed table.
Incorrect answer? Award **1 mark** for **three** correct answers.

Exam.Ninja

BLANK PAGE

KEY STAGE 2
ENGLISH READING

About the KS2 English Reading Practice Papers

There are three full sets of **KS2 English Reading Papers**.

Each set of KS2 English Reading Practice Papers consists of two separate booklets: a **Reading Booklet** and a **Reading Answer Booklet**.

Children are given a total of **60 minutes** to read the **three texts** within the Reading Booklet and use that information to answer all the questions within the Reading Answer Booklet. There are a maximum of **50 marks** available.

 This pencil sign means that an answer needs to be written either where indicated by the pencil or in the position instructed in the question.

Marking and Assessing the Papers

Once your child has completed a test, mark it using the **Answers and Mark Scheme** within this book, add up the marks to get a total out of **50** and enter them in the table below.

English Reading Marks Table

	SET A	SET B	SET C
Reading Answer Booklet (60 mins, out of 50)			

English Reading - Set A - Eating Insects

Q	Mark	Answers
1.	Up to 2	• Central and South America (accept South America or simply America) • Africa • Asia Award **2 marks** for listing **all three** of the above continents. Incorrect answer? Award **1 mark** for listing **any two** of the above.
2.	1	Tarantula
3.	1	Entomophagy
	1	Award **1 mark** to pupils that explain it as being a 'hot topic' because scientists are concerned with how to feed the world's growing population or because scientists believe it could be a solution to feeding a fast growing population (accept a similar explanation).
4.	Up to 2	• "We already use 70% of agricultural land to raise livestock" so there isn't enough land. • "Oceans are overfished," so we can't just increase fishing. • "Environments are becoming polluted," so it would cause excessive pollution. • "Climate change and disease threaten crop production," so farming land will become harder. Award **2 marks** for explaining how we can't just increase farming including **two** of the examples above. Incorrect answer? Award **1 mark** for a correct explanation that only includes **one** of the examples above. **Do not** award a mark if the pupil has not given any examples from the text or not directly related their example(s) to the question.
5.	1	• Sustainable • Nutritious • Potential jobs and income to people in poor areas. Award **1 mark** for answers that mention **all three** of the above points.
6.	1	Breed

Q	Mark	Answers
7.	Up to 2	Award **2 marks** to pupils that describe greenhouse gases as being harmful to the environment **and** that this will therefore affect how food can be farmed in the future if the environment remains (or gets increasingly) polluted (accept a similar explanation). Incorrect answer? Award **1 mark** to pupils that only state that greenhouse gases are harmful to the environment.
8.	Up to 2	Beef contains — 205g/kg of protein House crickets contain — 256g/kg of protein Locusts contain — than pork Mealworms contain the same omega-3 — 6mg/100g of iron Mealworms contain more omega-3 — 20mg/100g of iron Termites can contain — as fish Beef contains — 64% protein Award **2 marks** for correctly linking **all** of the statements. Incorrect answer? Award **1 mark** if there are **three** correctly linked statements.
9.	Up to 2	• "They can offer employment and generate cash income through the sale of the produce," meaning farmers can make money and be able to offer jobs to others. • "It also doesn't require a lot of experience or sophisticated equipment," meaning it could be simple for many people to quickly set up. • "Individuals can participate in these activities including women and those living in rural or urban areas that are lacking in available land," meaning that even people with not much land or space can take up insect farming. Award **2 marks** for correctly explaining why communities would want to rear and sell insects including **two** of the examples above. Incorrect answer? Award **1 mark** for a correct explanation that only includes **one** of the examples above. **Do not** award a mark if the pupil has not given any examples from the text or not directly related their example(s) to the question.

Q	Mark	Answers
10.	1	*Award **1 mark** to pupils whose answer states that it's surprising because the text states they have a foul odour (accept a similar explanation).*
11.	1	*Award **1 mark** to pupils whose answer explains that it's so we find the idea of eating insects more appealing or that we don't feel overly sick or unfamiliar about the idea of eating insects (accept a similar explanation).*
12.	1	*Award **1 mark** to pupils whose answer indicates that by using subheadings, the author is trying to make the information clearer, easier or faster to read or understand.*

English Reading - Set A - Adventures with Pip

Q	Mark	Answers
13.	1	A horse
14.	1	• Bit • Reins • Downy nostrils • Rubbery lips • Rearing • Hooves *Award **1 mark** to pupils that list **any two** of the above.*
15.	1	Prepared for
16.	Up to 2	• Cover distances that the author could not easily cover themselves. • Explore places rarely visited by humans. • Derive a feeling of complete freedom. *Award **2 marks** for correctly describing **two** of the above opportunities.* *Incorrect answer? Award **1 mark** for correctly describing one of the above.*
17.	1	*Award **1 mark** to pupils whose answer indicates that the path was overgrown because dog walkers or cyclists rarely used it (accept a similar explanation).*
18.	1	Penetrate

Q	Mark	Answers
19.	1	Spooked
20.	Up to 2	The author says 'so much for trust!' at the end of the text because (earlier in the text) the author stated that '**I trusted her with my life, and she trusted me with hers.**' Pip has now left the author alone (which is breaking this trust) and the author acknowledges this by stating 'so much for trust!' *Award **2 marks** for correctly explaining **why** the author says 'so much for trust!' **and** for including the correct example from the text.* *Incorrect answer? Award **1 mark** for pupils that correctly explain **why** the author says 'so much for trust' **but do not** include the correct example from the text.*
21.	Up to 2	The author suspected that the snake was an escaped pet because it was '**simply huge**' and '**rather exotic looking**' and was therefore not the type of snake that would naturally live in the wild in the English countryside. *Award **2 marks** for correctly explaining **why** the author suspected the snake was an escaped pet **and** for including the **two** examples from the text.* *Incorrect answer? Award **1 mark** for pupils that correctly explain why the author suspected the snake was an escaped pet but only includes **one** of the examples from the text.* ***Do not** award a mark if the pupil has not given any examples from the text or not directly related their example(s) to the question.*
22.	1	*Award **1 mark** to pupils whose answer suggests that the noise Pip made was described as 'terrifying' because it was the '**strangest sound**' the author had ever heard and entirely **unexpected**. Since Pip was spooked it is likely to have scared the author and been a noise of terror.*
23.	1	*Award **1 mark** to pupils whose answer indicates that Pip's hooves were punching the air violently and she was rearing high so it would have been too difficult, dangerous or frightening to get close and calm her down.*

Q	Mark	Answers
24.	Up to 2	'**Adventures with Pip**' is written in the **first person** because the author uses words like 'I, we and my' instead of 'his or her,' as shown by: • 'I turned back to where the rustling came from.' • 'I sat on a log and took an apple out of my bag.' • 'The feeling I get during this moment is always the most exhilarating rush.' • 'Now **we** were at the top, looking out over the undulating fields of brilliant yellows and greens.' *Award **2 marks** for correctly explaining that the text is written in the first person and for including **two** relevant examples from the text (such as those listed above).* *Incorrect answer? Award **1 mark** for pupils that explain that the text is written in the first person but only include **one** relevant example from the text to support their answer.* ***Do not** award a mark if the pupil has not given examples from the text or not directly related their example(s) to the question.*

English Reading - Set A - Elon Musk

Q	Mark	Answers
25.	1	*The **second** option:* Elon Musk is a wealthy entrepreneur who sold his first creation at the age of 12 and plans to colonise Mars.
26.	1	Successful
27.	1	*Award **1 mark** to pupils whose answer suggests that it seems exceptionally risky, unlikely to work, overly complicated or simply unbelievable seeing as humans have never managed to visit Mars (accept similar explanations).*

Q	Mark	Answers
28.	Up to 2	

Statement	Fact	Opinion
"If you haven't heard of him yet, you're in for a treat!"		✔
PayPal was sold to Ebay in 2002	✔	
Crazy, right?		✔

Award **2 marks** for the correctly stating whether **all three** statements were fact or opinion. Incorrect answer? Award **1 mark** if there are **two** correct statements.

29.	1	Gas-guzzling
30.	1	Award **1 mark** to pupils whose answer indicates that NASA invested in SpaceX after their fourth launch was a success.
31.	1	Daimler
32.	1	Earthshaking success
33.	Up to 2	

Statement	True	False
SpaceX has launched 20 rockets into space and is working on a large rocket to transport 100 people to Mars at a time.	✔	
Only five rocket launching teams have managed to send a rocket to Mars and back.		✔
The Tesla company is building a huge factory which will triple the world's yearly production of batteries.		✔
SolarCity achieved its goal of increasing the consumption of renewable energy in the U.S.	✔	

Award **2 marks** for the correctly stating whether **all four** statements were true or false. Incorrect answer? Award **1 mark** if there are **two** correctly ticked statements.

34.	1	'In true Elon style.'

Q	Mark	Answers
35.	Up to 2	This text is **'fact'** because it is an autobiographical piece for Elon Musk, a successful businessman. The text contains numerous sentences that are written as fact and not opinion, demonstrating that the text is factual. Examples of this include (but are not limited to): • 'He graduated with two degrees.' • 'In 1999, he sold his Zip2 for $307 million.' • 'At the age of 17 he went to work on a relative's farm in Canada.' • 'SpaceX has now successfully launched 20 times and NASA is a regular client.' *Award **2 marks** for correctly explaining that the text is a factual piece and for including **two** relevant examples from the text (such as those listed above).* *Incorrect answer? Award **1 mark** for pupils that explain that the text is a factual piece but only include **one** relevant example from the text to support their answer.* ***Do not** award a mark if the pupil has not given any examples from the text or not directly related their example(s) to the question.*
36.	Up to 2	The author is **impressed** with Elon's achievements. There are several examples of this within the text including (but not limited to) : • Musk being described as 'only 39 years old' and having many successful businesses. • Musk being described as 'only 12 years old' when he sold his first piece of software. • 'He could have taken his millions and lived a life of luxury on a private island but instead he risked it all in an attempt to create a better world for us all.' • 'He managed to set up all of these companies in just the four years following the PayPal sale!' • 'It'll be interesting to see what he comes up with next!' *Award **2 marks** for correctly explaining that the author is impressed with Musk's achievements **and** for including **two** relevant examples from the (such as those listed above).* *Incorrect answer? Award **1 mark** for pupils that explain that the author is impressed with Musk's achievements but only include **one** relevant example from the text.* ***Do not** award a mark if the pupil has not given any examples from the text or not directly related their example(s) to the question.*

English Reading - Set B - Bees

Q	Mark	Answers
1.	1	*The **second** option:* Bees like to live in arid places but not in high altitudes.
2.	1	*The **fourth** option:* Cross-pollination
3.	1	*Award **1 mark** to pupils that explain how important bees are to humans because they help pollinate many of the fruits and vegetables that we eat and that without bees these crops may cease to exist (accept a similar explanation).*
4.	1	Exploited
5.	1	Honey bee queens are replaced if they don't produce enough eggs.
6.	1	*Award **1 mark** to pupils whose answer explains that worker bees born in the spring are busier as there are lots of larvae to feed, whereas in autumn there are no larvae because the queen stops producing eggs at this time of year (accept similar explanations).*
7.	1	The **second** option: *Drones are male and do not live through the winter. Some workers stay to keep the queen warm in the winter.*
8.	Up to 2	• Honey bee queens can live up to 3 to 4 years, whereas the bumble bee queen will live up to 1 year. • Some bees stay with the honey bee queen over winter, however the bumble bee queen hibernates alone, whilst the rest of the colony dies. *Award **2 marks** for correctly listing **both** of the above differences.* *Incorrect answer? Award **1 mark** if a pupil has listed **one** of the above differences.*
9.	1	Alone *(accept synonyms such as 'by themselves'.)*
10.	1	Entomologists
11.	1	*Award **1 mark** to pupils that explain that 'Causes of CCD' has been shown in a flow diagram because it helps to simplify the information, make it clearer or make it easier to understand (accept similar explanations).*
12.	1	*Award **1 mark** to pupils whose answer describes that as a result of monoculture farming, bees become malnourished due to a limited diet of one type of pollen (accept similar explanations).*

Q	Mark	Answers
13.	Up to 2	*'Bees'* is a non-fiction piece because it is a scientific report with clear subheadings that's full of facts and statements about bees. There is no narrative or story. Examples of these facts include (but are not limited to): • 'There are 25,000 different types of bees in the world.' • 'They can range in size from 2mm to 4cm.' • 'The average honey bee can visit more than 2,000 flowers in one day.' • 'Workers born during the spring or summer months may live for 6 or 7 weeks.' *Award **2 marks** for correctly explaining that the text is a non-fiction piece and for including **two** relevant examples from the text (such as those listed above).* *Incorrect answer? Award **1 mark** to pupils that explain that the text is a non-fiction piece but only include **one** relevant example from the text to support their answer.* ***Do not** award a mark if the pupil has not given any examples from the text or not directly related their example(s) to the question.*

English Reading - Set B - Forever Land

Q	Mark	Answers
14.	1	'Trembling' and 'uncertainty'. *Award **1 mark** to pupils that list **both** of the above.*
15.	Up to 2	The author has avoided the use of the word 'walked' because it is a very descriptive piece and 'walked' does not tell the reader much about how Laurel and Fred were moving. Instead the author uses the emotive and descriptive verbs **'traipsing'**, **'trudging'** and **'battling'** to suggest they were tired, fed up and slowly making their way through the woodland. *Award **2 marks** for correctly explaining why the author has avoided using the word 'walked' and listing **two** of the above verbs.* *Incorrect answer? Award **1 mark** for correctly explaining why the author has avoided using the word 'walked' and only listed **one** of the above verbs.* ***Do not** award a mark if the pupil has not given any example verbs from the text or not directly related their use to the question.*
16.	1	*Award **1 mark** to pupils whose answer indicates that the word 'breathless' helps personify the leaves, suggesting that the area is lifeless and creating a dark and scary atmosphere (accept similar explanations).*

Exam.Ninja

Q	Mark	Answers
17.	1	• Incredible • Heavy • Yellow (accept 'yellow mass') • Close • Bright Award **1 mark** to pupils that list **any three** of the above.
18.	1	Award **1 mark** to answers that suggest Fred's concerned for his safety, that something awful might be in the cave (or happen to him) or that he may never come back (accept similar suggestions).
19.	1	Award **1 mark** to answers that identify that Fred puts his jumper up over his nose because there was 'an unrecognisable smell' in the cave (accept similar explanations).
20.	1	The **second** option: That they are physically tired.
21.	1	The **first** option: Studied
22.	1	Award **1 mark** to pupils that identify the author as describing the roots of the tree as the cave is at the bottom of a 'giant tree trunk'.
23.	1	Award **1 mark** to pupils whose answer indicates that the children knew they were standing in front of the correct door because they knew the correct door had a water symbol on it (accept similar explanations).
24.	1	• Cold • Tiredness • Doubt • Dread Award **1 mark** to pupils that list **all four** of the above.
25.	1	Award **1 mark** to pupils that describe the children as hoping to find 'the kingdom' with 'a beautiful community of creatures' behind the door (accept similar descriptions).

Q	Mark	Answers
26.	Up to 2	*'Forever Land'* takes place at night because the author describes Fred looking **'up one last time at the incredible moon'** and also that they had been walking **'for the last twelve hours.'** Award **2 mark**s to pupils that explain **'Forever Land'** as taking place at night **and** include **both** of the relevant examples above. *Incorrect answer?* Award **1 mark** to pupils that explain **'Forever Land'** as taking place at night **and** include **one** of the relevant examples above. **Do not** award a mark if the pupil has not given any examples from the text or not directly related their example(s) to the question.

English Reading - Set B - Unknown Killers within the Victorian Home

Q	Mark	Answers
27.	1	• Victorians could now more readily **access** fashionable products. • Victorians could more easily **afford** fashionable products. *Award **1 mark** to pupils that list **both** of the above.*
28.	1	*Award **1 mark** to pupils that describe Victorian manufacturers as being more concerned about production and profit rather than safety (accept similar explanations).*
29.	1	Arsenic
30.	Up to 2	• Wallpaper • Curtains • Dresses • Face powders • Children's sweets (accept sweets) *Award **2 marks** to pupils that list **all five** of the above.* *Incorrect answer?* Award **1 mark** to pupils that list **three** of the above.
31.	Up to 2	*Award **1 mark** to pupils that describe the significant popularity among middle-class Victorians of fashionable wallpapers and dyes and that these would not have been available were arsenic banned (accept similar explanations).* *Award **a further 1 mark** to pupils that also describe Victorian manufacturers being more interested in profits and production than the safety of their customers (or workers).*

Exam Ninja

Q	Mark	Answers
32.	1	Award **1 mark** to pupils that identify lead-painted toys as being appealing to children because they have a sweet taste.
33.	1	Award **1 mark** to pupils that describe lead poisoning as attacking the nervous system, affecting the brain and therefore impacting a child's development (accept similar explanations).
34.	1	• Lungs • Liver • Uterus Award **1 mark** to pupils that list **all three** of the above.
35.	1	The **second** option: Tightness
36.	1	Award **1 mark** to pupils that describe women as continuing to wear corsets because it was fashionable (accept similar explanations).
37.	Up to 2	The author **does not** approve of corsets. This is evidenced by: • The author asking why women would subject themselves to "this kind of torture" • The author stating that wearing corsets was "unfortunately" all in the name of fashion. Award **2 marks** for correctly explaining that the author disapproves of corsets and listing **both** of the above examples. Incorrect answer? Award **1 mark** for correctly explaining that the author does not approve of corsets and listing **one** of the above examples. **Do not** award a mark if the pupil has not given either of the examples from the text or not directly related their use to the question.
38.	Up to 2	In order to prevent a stove from exploding, you need to ensure they are fitted with **stopcocks** and **pressure valves**. The early stove designs made by the late Victorians were not fitted with these and so they were extremely **hazardous**. Award **2 marks** for correctly completing the sentences as above. Incorrect answer? Award **1 mark** for correctly completing **one** of the sentences as above.

Q	Mark	Answers
39.	Up to 2	Gas lights were dangerous at night because when they were turned off, the flame would go out but the gas could still leak through into the rooms, poisoning and suffocating people in their sleep (accept similar explanations). *Award **2 marks** for explaining that the gas would continue to flow after the flame had gone out **and** that it was poisonous and could cause suffocation.* *Incorrect answer? Award **1 mark** to pupils that only describe gas as being poisonous or causing suffocation but don't relate it to gas lighting.*
40.	Up to 2	**'Unknown Killers within the Victorian Home'** is **not** a persuasive text because, across the whole piece, the author is not trying to influence or change the opinion of the reader. It does not begin with a question, opinion or clear argument from the author. Instead, it gives us factual information relating to the past. Examples of these facts include (but are not limited to): • 'Throughout history there have been many unknown or hidden killers in the home.' • 'Two rich green colours known as 'Scheele's Green' and 'Paris Green' were the pinnacle of fashion at the time.' • 'Arsenic was also found in many dyes which were used on fabrics such as curtains, dresses, face powders and even in children's sweets!' • 'Even mild lead poisoning can cause an attack on the nervous system, affecting the brain and therefore, a child's development.' • 'It was the height of Victorian fashion to have the smallest possible waist, creating an hourglass figure.' *Award **2 marks** for correctly explaining that the text is not persuasive **and** for including **two** relevant examples from the text (such as those listed above).* *Incorrect answer? Award **1 mark** for correctly explaining that the text is not persuasive **and** for including **one** relevant example from the text.* ***Do not** award a mark if the pupil has not given any examples from the text or not directly related their use to the question.*

English Reading - Set C - Our Pet Wolves

Q	Mark	Answers
1.	1	*The **first** option:* Symbiotic
2.	1	*Award **1 mark** to pupils that identify the author mentioning that nearly all domestic dogs have been traced back to only three female wolves.*
3.	1	*The **fourth** option:* 35,000 years ago.
4.	Up to 2	• Dogs have learned to make eye contact with humans, which is not something that they would do with their own kind. • Pet dogs choose to run to their owners when they're scared, unlike other animals which normally run away. *Award **2 marks** for correctly describing **both** of the above examples.* *Incorrect answer? Award **1 mark** if a pupil has described **one** of the above examples.*
5.	1	*Award **1 mark** to pupils that explain that it's hard to know exactly what a dog is thinking because we are unable to communicate through speech (accept similar explanations).*
6.	Up to 2	*Award **2 marks** to pupils whose answer describes the 'reward' part of the brain as being highlighted when exposed to human scent **and** that this tells us the dog feels happy, positive emotions (accept synonyms) towards us.* *Incorrect answer? Award **1 mark** if a pupil has described the 'reward' part of the brain as being highlighted.*
7.	1	*Award **1 mark** to pupils that explain the Budapest experiment as being unsurprising because we already know that dogs feel positive emotions (accept synonyms) towards humans, evident from how they have developed a good relationship over time (accept similar explanations).*
8.	1	*Award **1 mark** to pupils that **agree** that the Massachusetts experiment **does** indeed show evidence that humans feel equal emotion towards their children and their pet dogs because the mothers tested produced a similar brain activity when exposed to each of their photographs.*

Q	Mark	Answers
9.	1	• A farmer and his (or her) sheepdog. • Guide dogs for the blind. *Award **1 mark** to pupils that describe **both** of the above examples of our successful relationship with dogs.*

10. Up to 2

	Fact	Opinion
"The wolf bone was found in the Taimyr Peninsula in Siberia."	✔	
"...dogs are also the only non-primates that look for eye contact with their human owners"	✔	
" It would be almost impossible to imagine a world without them."		✔

*Award **2 marks** for the correctly stating whether **all three** statements were fact or opinion. Incorrect answer? Award **1 mark** if there is **one** correct statement.*

11. Up to 2

'Our Pet Wolves' is a piece of **factual** writing because it describes the history of man's relationship with wolves and dogs and includes plenty of facts and statements. There is no narrative or story.

Examples of these facts include (but are not limited to):
- 'the Taimyr Wolf has passed on many of its genes to the Siberian Husky'
- 'there are an estimated 8.5 million pet dogs in the UK.'
- 'Scientists have now discovered a Taimyr wolf bone that is at least 35,000 years old.'
- 'Dogs are also the only non primates that look for eye contact with their human owners; something which scientists have discovered they don't even do with their biological parents!'

*Award **2 marks** for correctly explaining that the text is a factual piece **and** for including **two** relevant examples from the text (such as those listed above).*
*Incorrect answer? Award **1 mark** to pupils that explain that the text is a factual piece but only include **one** relevant example from the text to support their answer.*
***Do not** award a mark if the pupil has not given any examples from the text or not directly related their example(s) to the question.*

English Reading - Set C - Camping

Q	Mark	Answers
12.	1	• Going to school. • Eating meals. • Doing her homework. • Waking up. • Bedtime. *Award **1 mark** to pupils that list **any three** of the above things the author did every day in their childhood.*
13.	1	*Award **1 mark** to pupils that explain the author as having used the term 'such a treat' because it felt like she was breaking the rules as it was different to her normal routine (accept similar explanations).*
14.	1	*The **second** option:* Progressed
15.	1	*Award **1 mark** to pupils that explain that both fear and excitement can cause your body to react in the same way, which is that your heart pumps faster, you become more alert and your senses are heightened.*
16.	1	*Award **1 mark** to pupils that explain the word 'coincidentally' as being used because the author is talking about camping and she happened to meet her friend Amandine on a camping trip, which is a coincidence (accept similar explanations).*
17.	1	The author used the musty blanket that was between the saddle and the camel's back.
18.	1	*Award **1 mark** to answers that suggest that the group weren't prepared for it to rain because it was very unusual for it to rain in the Sahara in Morocco at that time of the year (accept similar suggestions).*
19.	1	The author would wake up at dawn and watch the sunrise.
20.	1	*Award **1 mark** to answers that explain the author's trip being so memorable because it was not easy or comfortable and she got satisfaction from surviving it (accept similar explanations).*
21.	1	*Award **1 mark** to pupils that explain the word 'smug' as being used because although her tent was heavy and old, it was the only one left standing in the heavy rain.*

Q	Mark	Answers
22.	Up to 2	

	Fact	Opinion
The thick blue and orange canvas had been newly waterproofed.	✔	
It seems rather dull now but at the time it was the best fun.		✔
We'd decided to take a bus to the edge of the Sahara where we proceeded to ride into the desert on camel back.	✔	

*Award **2 marks** for the correctly stating whether **all three** statements were fact or opinion. Incorrect answer? Award **1 mark** if there are **two** correct statements.*

| 23. | Up to 2 | By using the phrase 'a home from home,' the author means that you need to create a comfortable place like a home and do the same things that you would normally do at home. |

The examples that are mentioned within the text are:
- 'Access water.'
- 'Do the washing up.'
- 'A way to cook.'
- 'Create warmth.'
- 'Bathe.'

*Award **2 marks** for correctly explaining what the author meant in using 'a home from home' and giving **any two** of the above examples.*
*Incorrect answer? Award **1 mark** for correctly explaining what the author meant in using 'a home from home' and giving **one** of the above examples.*
***Do not** award a mark if the pupil has not given any examples from the text or has not directly related their use to the question.*

| 24. | 1 | *Award **1 mark** to pupils that describe the author as asking this question because she's trying to get the reader to understand that camping is about experiences away from modern technology, away from worrying about what other people are doing (accept similar explanations).* |

Q	Mark	Answers
25.	Up to 2	The author **likes** and **enjoys** camping. Even though it states in the text that she didn't like the desert spiders and the rain in Morocco, there are a number of examples that clearly demonstrate that these negative experiences do not detract from her enjoyment of camping. Examples of these facts include (but are not limited to): • 'My love for camping all started at a very young age.' • 'As an adult I still love camping, the idea of it still gets me so excited.' • 'I've never been so happy as when I finally saw our campsite of white canvas tents.' • 'You have to find solutions to otherwise easy problems (like where to go to the loo for instance!) and therefore, I find life becomes a lot more satisfying.' *Award **2 marks** to pupils that explain the author enjoys camping **and** include **two** relevant examples from the text (such as those listed above).* *Incorrect answer? Award **1 mark** for explaining that the author enjoys camping **and** for including one relevant example from the text.* ***Do not** award a mark if the pupil has not given any examples from the text or not directly related their use to the question.*

English Reading - Set C - Sugar

Q	Mark	Answers
26.	1	• Fruit • Vegetables • Dairy food *Award **1 mark** to pupils that list **all three** of the above food types where sugar is found naturally.*
27.	1	**Nine** different types of sugar.
28.	1	**Seven** teaspoons of sugar.
29.	1	*The **second** option:* Around 26,000 children aged 5 to 9 were admitted to hospital with tooth decay in 2013-14.

Q	Mark	Answers
30.	1	*The **second** option:* Result
31.	1	*Award **1 mark** to pupils that explain children as having to wait so long for an anaesthetic because there are so many children that are in need of treatment that hospitals are struggling to manage it.*
32.	1	Insulin
33.	1	As child obesity rises so does ⟶ tooth decay. Overweight people are more likely to develop ⟶ child diabetes. The government needs to invest in better education around ⟶ type 2 diabetes. *Award **1 mark** for correctly linking all of the statements.*
34.	Up to 2	The **principle** reason that the author has chosen to include the survey is to help support (or better understand) their claim that 'as we have seen the number of obese children rise, we have seen a rise in child diabetes' (accept similar explanations). A **further** reason for the survey's inclusion is to provide deeper factual details that may be of interest to the reader, such as whether more girls or boys had diabetes or the average age children contracted it (accept similar explanations). *Award **2 marks** to pupils that explain the principle reason **and** the further reason for why the survey was included.* *Incorrect answer? Award **1 mark** to pupils that explain the principle reason for why the survey was included.*
35.	1	*People with type 2 diabetes have problems with their feet due to poor circulation **and** lack of sensation.*
36.	1	*The **second** option:* Removed

Q	Mark	Answers
37.	Up to 2	• 'Devastating impact' on people's lives. • The further 'psychological impact'. • The additional risk that 'most people die within five years of their operation'. *Award **2 marks** to pupils that list **any two** of the above for the huge concern in rising numbers of amputations in the UK.* *Incorrect answer? Award **1 mark** for listing **one** of the above.* ***Do not** award a mark if the pupil has not given any examples from the text or not directly related their use to the question.*
38.	Up to 2	A relaxed attitude towards sugar could be damaging because: • It 'encourages over indulgence in children' which can lead to childhood obesity and diabetes. • It 'ignores the problem of tooth decay' which could lead to possible emergency dental treatment. *Award **2 marks** to pupils that describe **both** of the above reasons why a relaxed attitude to sugar could be dangerous **and** include the examples from the text.* *Incorrect answer? Award **1 mark** to pupils that describe **one** of the reasons above **and** includes the relevant example from the text.* ***Do not** award a mark if the pupil has not given any examples from the text or not directly related their use to the question.*

Q	Mark	Answers
39.	Up to 2	*'Sugar'* is a persuasive text because the author begins the text with a clear viewpoint by questioning our sugar consumption. She then includes facts, evidence, quotes and emotive words to support her own viewpoint that eating too much sugar is bad for you. Examples that *'Sugar'* is a persuasive text include (but are not limited to): • 'Dental decay can be a terrifying problem' as children may require emergency dental treatment. • 'I don't think many would choose to have all their teeth pulled out!' an opinion on choosing to continue to eat excessive sugar. • Choosing to include the following quote from Professor Hunt: 'During that time that child will be in pain, suffering and perhaps having repeated antibiotics.' • 'Many will have to face much more severe consequences ' if they have a severe case of type 2 diabetes. • *'Sugar'* also offers no open discussion that eating too much sugar could be a good thing (like a discussion text would.) *Award **2 marks** for explaining that the text is a persuasive text **and** for including **two** relevant examples from the text (such as those listed above).* *Incorrect answer? Award **1 mark** for explaining that the text is a persuasive text **and** for including **one** relevant example from the text.* ***Do not** award a mark if the pupil has not given any examples from the text or not directly related their use to the question.*

BLANK PAGE

KEY STAGE 2

GRAMMAR, PUNCTUATION AND SPELLING

ANSWERS & MARK SCHEMES

About the Grammar, Punctuation and Spelling Practice Papers

There are three **full** sets of **KS2 Grammar, Punctuation and Spelling Practice Papers**.

Each set of KS2 Grammar, Punctuation and Spelling Practice Papers consists of two separate tasks: Paper 1 **(Questions)** and Paper 2 **(Spelling)**.

 This pencil sign means that an answer needs to be written either where indicated by the pencil or in the position instructed in the question.

Paper 1 (Questions)

Paper 1 of the Grammar, Punctuation and Spelling Test is the Questions task. This lasts for **45 minutes** and has a total of **50 marks**.

Paper 2 (Spelling)

Paper 2 is the Spelling Task, an **audible test**. This lasts for approximately **20 minutes** and has a total of **20 marks**. For information about how to administer the Spelling Task including the instructions, transcripts and where to download the **FREE** audio, see page **79**.

Marking and Assessing the Papers

Once your child has completed a test, mark it using the **Answers and Mark Scheme** within this book. Note: in order to mark **Paper 2 (Spelling)**, use the transcripts on page **79**.

Add up the marks and write them in the table below. After completing a full set of papers, add up the scores for Paper 1 (Questions) and Paper 2 (Spelling) to get a total out of **70**.

Grammar, Punctuation and Spelling Marks Table

	SET A	SET B	SET C
Paper 1 (Questions) (45 mins, out of 50)			
Paper 2 (Spelling) (20 mins, out of 20)			
Total (out of 70)			

Q	Mark	Answers
1.	1	*The **second** option:* was, was
2.	1	*The **third** option:* Used properly, commas make the meaning of sentences clear.
3.	Up to 2	In — edible Non — sense Ir — regular Im — possible Dis — similar *Award **2 marks** for correctly linking **all** of the prefixes.* *Incorrect answer? Award **1 mark** for correctly linking **three** prefixes.*
4.	1	*While I <u>was writing</u> the story, my brother <u>was drawing</u> a picture.*
5.	1	*I <u>shan't</u> be able to attend the concert.*
6.	1	*The **second** option:* The boys hurried, as they didn't want to be late.
7.	1	*The **fourth** option:* Guy thought that Bath's streets were wonderful with all the old buildings.
8.	1	*<u>As</u> it is raining you can play <u>or</u> read indoors <u>but</u> you must not disturb your father.*
9.	1	*If <u>you</u> need to accompany <u>her</u> to the appointment, <u>I</u> will have to do it <u>myself</u>.*
10.	1	*The **fourth** option:* Species
11.	1	*The <u>courageous</u> fireman tackled the blaze singlehanded.*
12.	1	*Semi-colon*

Q	Mark	Answers

13. Up to 2

Sentence	Certainty	Possibility
I won't be able to come on Saturday.	✔	
He can't see you right now.	✔	
The train might wait at the station.		✔
You could leave it outside.		✔

Award **2 marks** for correctly stating **all** of the modal verb forms.
Incorrect answer? Award **1 mark** for correctly stating **two** of the modal verb forms.

14. 1 While we were there we sailed (along) the River Seine and climbed (up) the Eiffel Tower.

15. 1 Cyclists should always remain **stationary** while mounting their bicycle.
James needed to buy some more pencils from the **stationery** shop.

16. 1 The **fourth** option:
I wish you <u>were</u> able to take my place, but you have too little experience.

17. 1 Award **1 mark** to pupils whose answer indicates that the second sentence implies 'time travellers' feel a map is all they need whereas the first sentence implies 'travellers' feel a map is all they need. Therefore the comma alters the subject of the sentence.

18. 1 To get the (most) out of this exercise, you must put in (maximum) effort.

19. 1 Award **1 mark** to pupils that write a sentence that uses 'hard' as a adjective. For example:
  • 'The man picked up a hard rock.'
  • 'Mahogany and oak are hard woods.'

  1 Award **1 mark** to pupils that write a sentence that uses 'hard' as a adverb. For example:
  • 'The new employee worked very hard.'
  • 'She tried hard.'

20. 1 The **second** option:
Break

Q	Mark	Answers
21.	1	After leaving school, Sam headed off to play cricket.
22.	Up to 2	Transparent — Opaque Capture — Release Ebb — Flow Temporary — Permanent Award **2 marks** for correctly linking **all** of the antonyms. Incorrect answer? Award **1 mark** for correctly linking **two** antonyms.
23.	1	The **second** option: The agreement was signed by both parties.
24.	1	Simon ↑ S likes ↑ V cricket. ↑ O
25.	1	"<u>we</u> are going to <u>hastings</u> to visit the site of the famous battle where <u>william</u> the <u>conqueror</u> breached the <u>english</u> defence and took the throne of <u>england</u>," explained <u>george</u>.
26.	1	The <u>communication</u> system allows seals to conserve energy and avoid <u>unnecessary</u> fights during <u>breeding</u> season.
27.	1	The **first** option: The journey was long — longer than ever before — so we arrived home, exhausted.
28.	1	The **third** option: My Dad's car is old and dented.
29.	1	"Be quiet," the teacher told Sami. "Be quiet, Sami," said the teacher. Award **1 mark** for a direct speech sentence that's similar to either of the above examples.
30.	1	Henry VII (the first Tudor King of England) reigned from 1457 to 1509.

Exam.Ninja

Q	Mark	Answers
31.	Up to 2	

Sentence	Adverb	Adjective
He answered <u>correctly</u>.	✔	
He put the <u>correct</u> answer in the box.		✔
They offered some <u>friendly</u> advice.		✔
He drove the car <u>fast</u>- far too fast!	✔	

*Award **2 marks** for correctly stating whether **all** of the words were adverbs or adjectives.*
*Incorrect answer? Award **1 mark** for correctly stating **two** of the adverbs or adjectives.*

Q	Mark	Answers
32.	1	The **fourth** option: She gave an up-to-date account of the group's activities.
33.	1	The bus was hit by the express train as the train crossed the level crossing.
34.	Up to 2	

Sentence	Subordinating conjunction	Preposition
The children go to bed before eight o'clock.		✔
You should think before you make a decision.	✔	
They came to see us before Christmas.		✔

*Award **2 marks** for correctly stating **all** the uses of 'before'.*
*Incorrect answer? Award **1 mark** for correctly stating **two** of the uses of 'before'.*

Q	Mark	Answers
35.	Up to 2	

Noun	Adjective
Accident	Accidental
Expression	Expressionless
Wool	Woolly
Logic	Logical
Sympathy	Sympathetic

Award **2 marks** for correctly stating **all** the adjectives.
Incorrect answer? Award **1 mark** for correctly stating **two** of the adjectives.

---

36. Up to 2

Sentence	Subordinating conjunction	Coordinating conjunction
Sarah's sister lost her toy, <u>so</u> Sarah bought her another.		✔
James was late <u>because</u> he missed the train.	✔	
We must hurry <u>or</u> we will be late.		✔

Award **2 marks** for correctly stating **all** the conjunctions.
Incorrect answer? Award **1 mark** for correctly stating **two** of the conjunctions.

---

37. 1 — <u>The</u> doctor told Amy to take <u>one</u> pill <u>every</u> four hours.

38. 1 — Although <u>I have seen</u> the film twice already, I was pleased to hear that I will have the opportunity to see it again next week.

39. 1 — <u>A new film about the life and discoveries of Darwin</u> is planned for next year.

40. 1 — It is <u>mine</u>. (accept his, hers, yours, theirs, ours)

41. 1 — My brother passed the exam, <u>because he had revised very well</u>.
Award **1 mark** for writing a subordinate clause such as the above (i.e. a clause that's reliant on the main clause).

42. 1 — Before he went to bed, he did his homework.

Grammar, Punctuation & Spelling - Paper 1 (Questions) Set B Answers

Q	Mark	Answers
		Page 67 of 88
1.	**1**	*Daniel <u>was</u> seven last week.*
2.	**1**	*Use a capital letter at the <u>beginning</u> of a sentence.*
3.	**1**	*Last week I <u>was cleaning</u> out the garage while Oscar <u>was mending</u> the fence.*
4.	**Up to 2**	Dis — behave Mis — appear Im — perfect Un — necessary Non — fiction *Award **2 marks** for correctly linking **all** of the prefixes.* *Incorrect answer? Award **1 mark** for correctly linking **three** prefixes.*
5.	**1**	*While I was travelling to school, I learned the poem.*
6.	**1**	*The **fourth** option:* *After climbing the fence, we walked across the field.*
7.	**1**	*The **fourth** option:* *whenever*
8.	**1**	*He said it was <u>his</u>, but I know it is <u>mine</u>.*
9.	**1**	*The parcel <u>that my uncle sent</u> arrived on Saturday.*
10.	**1**	*The **first** option:* *Charles and Suraj found Rachel's books in the garden.*
11.	**1**	*The **fourth** option:* *Animals*

Q	Mark	Answers
12.	Up to 2	

Sentence	Subordinating conjunction	Preposition
We will wait **until** six o'clock.		✔
She will wait **until** he arrives.	✔	
I will wait **until** then		✔

Award **2 marks** for correctly stating **all** of the uses of 'until'.
Incorrect answer? Award **1 mark** for correctly stating **two** of the uses of 'until'.

Q	Mark	Answers
13.	1	Both Sally <u>and</u> Meg arrived on time <u>but</u> neither Jonathan <u>nor</u> Michael did.
14.	1	Semi-colon
15.	1	After she got <u>off</u> the bus, Lois realised she had left her folder <u>under</u> the seat. Panicking, she ran <u>towards</u> the bus stop and jumped <u>on</u> the <u>next</u> bus.
16.	1	The **fourth** option: were
17.	1	The <u>abandoned</u> building was <u>left</u> untouched since the first decade of the nineteenth century.
18.	1	Award **1 mark** to pupils whose answer indicates that the second sentence implies 'Paul' is being asked for help whereas the first sentence implies that someone is being asked to help 'Paul'. Therefore the comma changes 'Paul' from being the object to the subject of the sentence.
19.	1	Award **1 mark** to pupils that write a sentence that uses 'walk' as a noun. For example: • 'We went for a walk in the woods.' • 'The children embarked on a long and treacherous walk.'
	1	Award **1 mark** to pupils that write a sentence that uses 'walk' as a verb. For example: • 'I am going to walk into town.' • 'Ella missed the bus and had to walk home.'
20.	1	The **fourth** option: Carry

Q	Mark	Answers
21.	1	The men dug a ditch <u>before they started to build the well</u>. Award **1 mark** for writing a subordinate clause such as the above (i.e. a clause that's reliant on the main clause).
22.	Up to 2	Lead — Minute Immense — Minute Freedom — Captivity Commence — Conclude (Lead→Follow, Immense→Minute, Freedom→Captivity, Commence→Conclude) Award **2 marks** for correctly linking **all** of the antonyms. Incorrect answer? Award **1 mark** for correctly linking **two** antonyms.
23.	1	Have you got <u>any</u> batteries I could borrow?
24.	1	(jennifer)(small) lives at 17 (st)(peter's)(lane). (her) birthday is on 18ᵗʰ (may).
25.	1	Running at breakneck speed, Donald managed to win the race.
26.	1	• 100g of flour • One egg • 300ml of milk • One tablespoon of butter or margarine **Note:** The purpose of this exercise is simply to ensure that pupils can extract items from a list that's separated using commas. It is therefore perfectly acceptable for them to state either '1 egg' or 'One egg' and likewise '100g of flour' or simply '100g flour'.
27.	1	The **first** option: The first thing Rebecca did when she got to school — before she even took off her coat — was to find her friend, Laura.
28.	1	An exclamation mark is used at the end of this sentence in order to express surprise at the cat jumping onto Olivia's shoulder.
29.	1	A <u>huge</u> wave snatched the oar that we had decided to cling on to instead of joining the <u>crowded</u> boat and eventually we were swept to an <u>uninhabited</u> island.
30.	1	The **second** option: Fronted adverbial

Q	Mark	Answers
31.	1	The courageous boy made his way <u>carefully</u> along the ledge.
32.	1	The **fourth** option: Sarah jumped into the boat.
33.	1	The **second** option: Amy was learning her spellings.
34.	1	"Remember to come straight home, Luke," said Luke's mother. Award **1 mark** to pupils that write a sentence such as the above and uses speech marks correctly.
35.	Up to 2	

Noun	Adjective
Beauty	Beautiful
Courage	Courageous
Fortune	Fortunate
Energy	Energetic
Disaster	Disastrous

Award **2 marks** for correctly stating **all** the adjectives.
Incorrect answer? Award **1 mark** for correctly stating **two** of the adjectives.

Q	Mark	Answers
36.	1	The **first** option: After many nasty scrapes (and minus his socks and shoes) the naughty boy eventually arrived home to a severe telling-off.

Q	Mark	Answers
37.	Up to 2	

Sentence	Subordinating conjunction	Coordinating conjunction
We have raspberries <u>or</u> strawberries.		✔
We have raspberries <u>because</u> there are no strawberries.	✔	
We can have raspberries <u>and</u> strawberries.		✔

*Award **2 marks** for correctly stating **all** the conjunctions.*
*Incorrect answer? Award **1 mark** for correctly stating **two** of the conjunctions.*

Q	Mark	Answers
38.	1	Although Mrs Johnson <u>has lived</u> in London for thirty years, she was born in Scotland and she would like to return to live there one day.
39.	1	She has given all of <u>her</u> books to him because she doesn't need them anymore.
40.	1	Connor has three hobbies**:** playing basket ball, performing magic tricks and writing computer programs.
41.	1	<u>The long, hot summer's day</u> eventually drew to an end.
42.	1	The boy hero was rewarded for his <u>bravery</u> many times during his <u>childhood</u>. He will be remembered for his courageous <u>attitude</u> in the face of <u>danger</u>.
43.	1	The boys' bicycles were stolen by the same thieves who had previously taken the girls' toys.
44.	1	The **fourth** option: Noun phrase

Grammar, Punctuation & Spelling - Paper 1 (Questions) Set C Answers

Q	Mark	Answers
1.	1	The **fourth** option: What is the answer.
2.	1	The **fourth** option: The railway <u>was</u> once the most popular form of transport, but now most people <u>have</u> cars.
3.	1	The **first** option: One of Jack's books has lost its cover.
4.	Up to 2	Mis — septic Ex — justice In — turn Re — understood Anti — change Award **2 marks** for correctly linking **all** of the prefixes. Incorrect answer? Award **1 mark** for correctly linking **three** prefixes.
5.	1	<u>He'd</u> forgotten the map.
6.	1	The police said that the accident <u>which happened last night</u> was unavoidable.
7.	Up to 2	<table><tr><th>Sentence</th><th>Certainty</th><th>Possibility</th></tr><tr><td>The ride might be too scary for you.</td><td></td><td>✔</td></tr><tr><td>It may rain later.</td><td></td><td>✔</td></tr><tr><td>I could sing at the concert.</td><td></td><td>✔</td></tr><tr><td>I won't break the rules again.</td><td>✔</td><td></td></tr></table> Award **2 marks** for correctly stating **all** of the modal verb forms. Incorrect answer? Award **1 mark** for correctly stating **two** of the modal verb forms.
8.	1	On <u>Wednesday</u> my <u>brother</u>, <u>Damien</u>, ran the <u>marathon</u> from <u>Sevenoaks</u> to <u>London</u> in an <u>hour</u>.
9.	1	<u>Almost all marsupials</u> are nocturnal, which means they are awake at night.
10.	1	The cabins on the cruise ship were really <u>luxurious</u>.

Q	Mark	Answers
11.	1	I haven't seen my friend since she returned <u>from</u> America <u>on</u> Monday.
12.	1	The **third** option: Semi-colon
13.	1	The **fourth** option: Relative clause
14.	1	Semi-colon

15. — Up to 2

Sentence	Main clause	Subordinate clause	Relative clause
Charlie, <u>who is in my class</u>, has won the dance championship.			✔
<u>Charlie practises every day</u>, after he gets home from school.	✔		
Charlie continued to dance when he'd twisted his ankle, <u>even though it hurt.</u>		✔	

Award **2 marks** for correctly classifying **all** of the clauses.
Incorrect answer? Award **1 mark** for correctly classifying **two** of the clauses.

Q	Mark	Answers
16.	1	The pretty village nestles <u>below</u> the hills <u>between</u> the river and the canal. Talyboat is a perfect place for hill-walking and gentle strolls <u>along</u> the canal or <u>through</u> the lowland countryside.
17.	1	General <u>fatigue</u> overtook the company and some collapsed through hunger or sheer <u>weariness</u>.
18.	1	<u>Although</u> he has never been to Sweden, Anthony speaks the language very well. She will not play in the orchestra <u>unless</u> she practises every day. <u>While</u> I was working, he crept out of the room.
19.	1	Award **1 mark** to pupils that write a sentence that uses 'dark' as a noun. For example: • Tom was sitting in the dark. • Peter couldn't find his way in the dark.

Q	Mark	Answers
20.	1	Award **1 mark** to pupils that write a sentence that uses 'dark' as an adjective. For example: • The dark night seemed to last forever. • Those clouds look awfully dark.
21.	Up to 2	Frequently — Rarely Disperse — Collect Private — Public Exterior — Interior Award **2 marks** for correctly linking **all** of the antonyms. Incorrect answer? Award **1 mark** for correctly linking **two** antonyms.
22.	1	**All** the sentences except '**The horse jumped the gate.**' are written in the passive voice.
23.	1	The shrew has a higher metabolic rate than any other animal↑ its heart beats eight hundred times a minute. ✓
24.	1	The first sentence is telling the reader that they already know it is polite to shake hands with someone, as it states 'you know it's polite,' however the second sentence is informing the reader for the first time that it is polite to shake hands with someone, as it states 'it's polite.' Award **1 mark** to pupils whose answer demonstrates that they have understood the difference between the two sentences.
25.	Up to 2	

Adverbs of time	Adverbs of place	Adverbs of manner
Tomorrow Before Last	Out There	Quickly Calmy Cautiously

Award **2 marks** for correctly placing **all** of the adverbs.
Incorrect answer? Award **1 mark** for correctly placing **four** adverbs.

Q	Mark	Answers
26.	1	I <u>have been</u> to London many times.

Q	Mark	Answers
27.	Up to 2	On Wednesday Philippa and Katriona received an award for bravery. ↑(P) ↑(P) ↑(P) ↑(C) ↑(A) Their outstanding courage was appreciated by the whole community. ↑(A) Award **2 marks** for correctly identifying **all** of the nouns. Incorrect answer? Award **1 mark** for correctly identifying **three** nouns.
28.	1	I telephoned to say that they'd left their ball at our house. Lauren's brother, David said it wasn't theirs and that he'd thought it was ours.
29.	Up to 2	<u>At last</u>, she reached home. <u>Before I knew it</u>, the ground gave way beneath my feet. Award **2 marks** for correctly underlining **both** fronted adverbials. Incorrect answer? Award **1 mark** for correctly underlining **one** fronted adverbial.
30.	Up to 2	"<u>Can</u> I go out to play?" "You really <u>should</u> finish your homework first." "I said I <u>might</u> take Alan to the park" "You <u>will</u> get into trouble if the work is not done." "I suppose I <u>could</u> meet him later." Award **2 marks** for correctly underlining **all** the modal verbs. Incorrect answer? Award **1 mark** for correctly underlining **three** modal verbs.
31.	1	A toad-like creature emerged from the shadows. The new kittens are house-trained already.
32.	Up to 2	Sarah Jones (shown on the left in the picture) is captain this year. When an animal hibernates (sleeps through the winter) its body temperature drops and its heart rate and breathing slow down. Award **2 marks** for correctly placing **both** sets of brackets. Incorrect answer? Award **1 mark** for correctly placing **one** set of brackets.
33.	1	Lynne asked the shopkeeper if she could reach the top shelf.

Q	Mark	Answers

34. | Up to 2 |

Noun	Adjective
Mess	Messy
Love	Lovely (or loveless)
Care	Careful (or careless)
Guilt	Guilty (or guiltless)

Award **2 marks** for correctly stating **all** the adjectives.
Incorrect answer? Award **1 mark** for correctly stating **two** of the adjectives.

35. | 1 | If he <u>were</u> a little more careful, he wouldn't keep breaking things!

36. | 1 | Is that the lady <u>whom</u> she met at the library?

37. | Up to 2 | Award **1 mark** to pupils whose example uses 'its' to refer to something that belongs to or is associated with something in the third person singular (that isn't a he or a she).
For example: 'its front door was wet' means the front door belonging to the object that 'its' refers to, was wet.
Award a further **1 mark** to pupils whose second example uses 'it's' as a contracted form of 'it is'. For example: 'It's the second of the month tomorrow!'

38. | 1 | Full of excitement, she began to open the parcel, but her smile soon faded when she realised what was inside.

39. | 1 | The **second** option:
rather than

BLANK PAGE

KEY STAGE 2
GRAMMAR, PUNCTUATION AND SPELLING

SPELLING TRANSCRIPTS

Using This Transcript

As part of buying this book you are entitled to download the audio for the **Spelling Papers** for **FREE** from:

http://www.ExamNinja.co.uk/audio

Simply go to the link and follow the instructions to download your audio.

We encourage you to use our recordings as they have been **professionally produced** to closely reflect those that children will face in the **real exam**. Simply play the relevant audio file and wait approximately 20 minutes until your child has finished the test.

In the event that you cannot use the audio files you should read aloud the following instructions:

- "Listen carefully to the instructions I am going to give you.

- I am going to read twenty sentences. Each sentence within your answer booklet has a word missing.

- You should listen carefully to the missing word and fill this in, making sure you spell it correctly.

- I will read the word, then the word within a sentence, then repeat the word a third time.

- You will not be able to ask questions once the test has begun so if you have any questions you may ask them now."

Answer any questions your child has. When they are ready to begin the test, tell them that you **will not** be able to answer **any** further questions or interrupt the test once you have started reading the questions.

The instructions and questions **must** be read out consistently. Start by stating the **question number** and **the word**, then **the word within a sentence** and finally **the word again**. Wait 10 seconds before asking the next question for your child to spell the word.

After the test has finished, remind children that they are **not allowed** to change their answers and that they should **remain seated** until their answer sheet has been collected.

Q	Answers
1	*The word is: Colour.* *The **colour** purple is made by mixing blue and red.*
2	*The word is: Awkward.* *An **awkward** move resulted in a twisted ankle.*
3	*The word is: Cease* *The children did not **cease** chatting all afternoon.*
4	*The word is: Fierce* *The **fierce** bear ripped the tent.*
5	*The word is: Minutes* *The class will begin in five **minutes**.*
6	*The word is: Accurate* *Is it possible to draw an **accurate** map?*
7	*The word is: Determined* *She was **determined** to succeed.*
8	*The word is: Scissors* *You will need tissue paper, glue and a pair of **scissors**.*
9	*The word is: Shriek* *Louise let out a **shriek** when she saw the crocodile.*
10	*The word is: Thoroughly* *The house needs to be cleaned **thoroughly**.*
11	*The word is: Surprise* *It was a huge **surprise** to be awarded first prize.*
12	*The word is: Extraordinary* *An **extraordinary** incident happened last night.*
13	*The word is: Fulfil* *Selina hopes to **fulfil** her ambition to be a vet.*

Q	Answers
14	*The word is: Separate* *The cook showed us how to **separate** the yolk from the white.*
15	*The word is: Occasionally* ***Occasionally** we walk to school.*
16	*The word is: Postponed* *Our annual cricket match was **postponed** because of bad weather.*
17	*The word is: Sufficient* *The expedition team left camp with **sufficient** supplies for five days.*
18	*The word is: Necessary* *It is **necessary** to make a good impression on your first day.*
19	*The word is: Committee* *The **committee** meets once a month.*
20	*The word is: Signature* *William wrote his **signature** at the bottom of the letter.*

Grammar, Punctuation & Spelling - Spelling Transcript : Set B

Q	Answers
1	*The word is: Noisy* *The teacher told the **noisy** children to be quiet.*
2	*The word is: Echoed* *The sound **echoed** through the building.*
3	*The word is: Weight* ***Weight** is often measured in grams and kilograms.*
4	*The word is: Carriage* *A horse and **carriage** waited outside the church.*
5	*The word is: Machinery* *Old **machinery** was removed from the disused factory.*
6	*The word is: Corridor* *Their classroom is at the end of the **corridor**.*
7	*The word is: Grateful* *David was very **grateful** for the unexpected gift.*
8	*The word is: Invisible* *The minute stitches were almost **invisible**.*
9	*The word is: Extinguish* *The fire crew managed to **extinguish** the blaze.*
10	*The word is: Absorb* *You can use a sponge to **absorb** the water.*
11	*The word is: Rehearsed* *Year six **rehearsed** in the hall after school.*
12	*The word is: Approximately* *It is **approximately** 120 kilometres from Dover to London.*
13	*The word is: Obedient* *Of all the dogs, the Labrador is the most **obedient**.*

Exam.Ninja

Q	Answers
14	*The word is: Suspicious* *Lana told the police that she had seen something **suspicious**.*
15	*The word is: Accommodate* *He asked if we could **accommodate** another guest.*
16	*The word is: Curiosity* *Max's natural **curiosity** often got him into trouble.*
17	*The word is: Interfere* *They have no right to **interfere** with our plans.*
18	*The word is: Rhyme* *Not all poems **rhyme**.*
19	*The word is: Sacrifice* *Could you **sacrifice** some of your spare time to help?*
20	*The word is: Government* *A new **government** was elected this year.*

Grammar, Punctuation & Spelling - Spelling Transcript : Set C

Q	Answers
1	*The word is: Castles* *The Normans built **castles** all over England.*
2	*The word is: Complete* *You should **complete** the task in fifty minutes.*
3	*The word is: Escaped* *Forty prisoners **escaped** by means of a tunnel.*
4	*The word is: Challenge* *Scott needed a new **challenge**, so he took up golf.*
5	*The word is: Pierce* *Luckily, the thorn didn't **pierce** Amy's skin.*
6	*The word is: Designed* *The new school was **designed** by a famous architect.*
7	*The word is: Tongue* *Jeremy recited the **tongue** twister.*
8	*The word is: Develop* *The world needs to **develop** renewable energy systems.*
9	*The word is: Envelope* *Justin placed the letter in the **envelope**.*
10	*The word is: Vehicle* *The police were able to trace the **vehicle** because Harry remembered the number plate.*
11	*The word is: Communicate* *You should try to **communicate** your ideas clearly.*
12	*The word is: Knowledge* *Travelling can broaden one's **knowledge** of the world.*
13	*The word is: Amateur* *Although only an **amateur**, he won many races.*

Q	Answers
14	*The word is: Parliament* *There are six hundred and fifty members of **Parliament**.*
15	*The word is: Legible* *The writing on the manuscript is faded but **legible**.*
16	*The word is: Equipped* *The caravan is **equipped** for four guests.*
17	*The word is: Environment* *We can help the **environment** by setting pollution limits.*
18	*The word is: Embarrassed* *Tony was very **embarrassed** by his mistake.*
19	*The word is: Privilege* *It was a huge **privilege** to be given the best seat.*
20	*The word is: Corresponds* *Lucy **corresponds** with her friend in Australia.*

NOTES

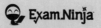